A NEW LEVEL MINDSET

AN ASPIRING ENTREPRENEUR RISING OUT

OF FEAR INTO GREATNESS

By Jessaca C. Rowe

BK Royston Publishing
P. O. Box 4321
Jeffersonville, IN 47131
502-802-5385
http://www.bkroystonpublishing.com
bkroystonpublishing@gmail.com

© Copyright – 2017

All Rights Reserved. No part of this book may be reproduced, stored in a retrieval system, or transmitted by any means without the written permission of the author.

Cover Design: Letrin F. Mattear by Articyoulate Creates.

ISBN: 978-1-946111-38-8

Printed in the United States of America

DEDICATION

I dedicate this book to those who aspire to become full-time entrepreneurs.

Success is worth the RISK! – Jessaca Rowe

ACKNOWLEDGMENTS

To my Husband Horace who has listened, supported and empathized with me on this journey. You have never doubted me and always encouraged me to push full speed ahead with my goals and dreams.

To my Children Terrance and Maleah. Your unconditional love is priceless. Thank you for assisting me on this journey when I needed you. Thank you for cheering me on when I thought writing this book wasn't possible.

To my Mother Linda and my Brother Walter. Thank you for those spontaneous family round table meetings. Sitting and talking with you has given me the motivation I needed to continue to push past my doubts and become a woman of courage and strength.

To my Sisters Danisha (RIP) and Qiana. Though I do not have biological sisters, you two have been there for me as if you were family. I appreciate your kindness, support and love over the years. I am thankful for the advice and encouragement you've given me, when I would feel as if I didn't have any strength left.

I love you ALL,

Jessaca

TABLE OF CONTENTS

DEDICATIONS	iii
ACKNOWLEDGMENTS	v
INTRODUCTION	ix
THE JOURNEY TO GREATNESS!	1
I NEED A GROWTH MINDSET	13
CONFIDENCE…UMM…YEAH I NEED THAT!	19
TIME TO DEVELOP CLARITY	27
FOCUS AND DISCIPLINE	33
THE POWER OF SUPPORT	41
READY…SET…GOALS!	49
CREATIVITY IS KEY!	57
BECOMING A RISK TAKER	61
READ!	69
SET BACKS HAPPEN FOR A COME BACK!	73
FINAL THOUGHTS	79

INTRODUCTION

WHY I WROTE THIS BOOK

There is a need for aspiring entrepreneurs to become fully aware of concepts and strategies needed to get to the next level of entrepreneurship. In my four years of studying of entrepreneurship, I realized that many aspiring entrepreneurs were not introduced to the mindset development stage of entrepreneurship. I've learned that entrepreneurship is a state of mind. In order to get to the point of building a thriving business, you must thrive in your mind first. Many people just jump into the world of entrepreneurship and don't become successful as they'd like in the amount of time they thought they would. Many startups fail within the first year. Often times, this is because the person was not mentally prepared to face the challenges that come with the journey. One must research and study their industry accordingly. They must put in the necessary efforts and be willing to take risks. I wrote this book to give aspiring entrepreneurs insight as to what it takes mentally to become a full-time successful entrepreneur.

A NEW LEVEL MINDSET

AN ASPIRING ENTREPRENEUR RISING OUT OF FEAR INTO GREATNESS

A New Level Mindset

The Journey to GREATNESS!

I went back to school in 2010 to complete my bachelor's degree. I majored in criminal justice because I was always intrigued with court cases and those scary murder mystery shows that came on cable. A year before graduation, I began looking for work. I was already working a full-time job at a law firm as a data entry clerk, but I was not happy. I knew there was more to life than just working in a cubicle. While I was studying criminal justice, I wasn't sure of the field I wanted to go into. One day in one of my classes, I overheard a conversation of two people. They too had been undecided on what field they wanted to work in after graduation. I asked if I could join their conversation. During our talk, one of them mentioned volunteer work. They explained that they had been told that volunteerism is a good place to start, if you were unable to decide on a career field. There is no hardcore commitment, and you could volunteer at many places as you like to get a feel of the different career industries; plus you'd be doing a good deed. I thought about it for a couple of days and decided to research nonprofit organizations in Los Angeles. As I was doing my research on volunteerism, I was careful to choose organizations that were aligned with subjects that caught my interest while I was in school. 'At-Risk Youths' happened to be on my radar. I learned that many children in certain

A New Level Mindset

neighborhoods were at risk of becoming involved in activities that could put them in a situation that would be difficult to get out of, in jail or dead. After volunteering at many at-risk youth organizations and actually loving it, I decided to study nonprofit management. It was a great experience to learn about what actually happens in the world of nonprofit organizations. Nonprofits are the glue that keeps many communities intact when government funds don't kick in as they should.

After graduating with a degree in criminal justice in 2013 and completing a nonprofit management certification, I struggled to find employment. I was upset and frustrated.

Jessaca C. Rowe

I had graduated from college with this 'big ole degree' and certificate in nonprofit management. I thought surely that having these credentials would easily get me in the door of a great career in criminal justice.

I went on countless interviews, constantly revising my resume and cover letters to fit the job descriptions and the whole nine, but it was not working out as I had planned. My thinking was, "You get a degree; you get a good job." After trying to figure out what was holding me back from getting a job that aligned with my degree, I realized that I only went back to school to get a degree. I wasn't focused on doing what I was passionate about, because I didn't know what I was passionate about. At that time, criminal justice and nonprofit organizations were my career interests, and I was ready to start working in at least one of these fields. I wanted to work with at-risk youth at a nonprofit organization in a capacity where I would be able to assist them with getting into college and providing them with the tools to finish college. But my dreams of doing this were not coming true as I had pictured. For six months, I dealt with anxiety and depression. This would be one of the darkest times in my life. I struggled on a daily basis to "feel better." I ended up in the E.R. for a couple of hours, because the pain of not starting work in my career field after graduation was so devastating. I was given anti-depression medication and a few days off work to help lessen the pain and suffering, but those were band-aids to cover a deep wound. I was struggling to heal.

One day, I decided that I was not going to allow this state of a bitter mind consume me and stress me out to the point where I would end up on my death bed. Soon, I figured out that I could no longer go on living in this state of mind. I had to change; level up and do better.

In April of 2014, I discovered Heal a Woman Heal a Nation (HWHN) on Facebook. It is an empowerment organization for women. After listening to many of their webinars and teleconferences, I decided to participate in their annual Unlimited You Conference in 2015 in

Baltimore. I thought of asking others to attend the conference with me, but I thought to myself, 'This was MY journey, and I needed to go alone. I needed to do some soul searching to find out who I truly was, what my gifts and talents were and how I could use them to help others. I learned from HWHN that I could use my skills to help others and work for myself. HUH? Work for myself? Wait a minute... I grew up knowing the standard of going to school, getting a job, retiring and being happy. Working for yourself...ummm...naw.... that's not possible, better yet that is not for me. In April of 2015, after two days of the conference in Baltimore, I was blown away. I began to work on planning to work for myself or as it is known, become an entrepreneur. I did heavy research to figure out the path I wanted to pursue. It was exhausting and scary, and I thought that I would never find my path. I took a break to regroup to figure this out. I learned that I would need a coach to help me pull all of the greatness out of me, so I could figure this out. There was a price associated with this; a price that I was not willing to pay. I wasn't ready mentally and financially to understand that I needed help from someone to get on the road to entrepreneurship, and actually pay them monies to teach me what I needed to know.

Another year passed by and nothing happened. I was still researching and studying

A New Level Mindset

entrepreneurship to find the resources I needed to get to started. It wasn't until I found the motivators of all motivators. I followed influencers such as Lisa Nicholas, Tony Robbins, Les Brown, Eric Thomas, Iyanla Vanzant and even Oprah, but nothing could prepare me for Ms. Dawniel Winningham – The Wealth Speaker. She was exactly who and what I needed to get myself on the right track. She fully explained through her Facebook Live and Periscope videos that the ticket to the next level of entrepreneurship was not free. I needed to pay someone who was experienced to help me reach the next level of entrepreneurship. She shared her story several times as I watched her on social media throughout the day. I even went to

YouTube, to find her earlier broadcasts. She helped me understand that my thinking was holding me back. She went on to say that, "A changed mindset can put you in places in your life that you've always dreamed of, but if you refuse to change your mind on the things you need to do to become an entrepreneur, you will remain stuck." WOW! OMG! Talk about a break through! WHEW! A sense of relief overcame me, and I broke down in tears. It was tears of joy. Once I discovered this, I did a lot of reminiscing on all the things I had gone through to obtain a job and to get on the path to entrepreneurship, and then it hit me! There were levels to this thing. There were steps that needed to be taken in order to get to the next level. I

A New Level Mindset

realized that I had to level up and go from having an employee mindset to an entrepreneur mindset.

After fully taking in the words of Ms. Dawniel Winningham, I soon discovered why so many don't make it to full time entrepreneurship. After watching countless live stream videos on Periscope and Facebook and reading the comments in those videos and in Facebook groups, I realized that people were simply just not prepared mentally; it was a mindset thing. Many people look at what other entrepreneurs have and don't understand the true thought process that goes into becoming a full-time entrepreneur, and I was one of them. I got back to doing more research, and discovered a number of necessary characteristics that aspiring

Jessaca C. Rowe

entrepreneurs needed in order to continue to get to a new level mindset.

Sit back and enjoy the remainder of this reading.

I promise, I'll get straight to the point.

I Need a Growth Mindset

Yep! I am ready! I am ready to put my all into becoming a successful entrepreneur! Or was I? As I continued my research into entrepreneurship, I came across people who were able to help me pursue this. Their helpful services would cost me and it was not cheap. The fees for business coaching range anywhere from $300-$500 a month or even more. Some coaches had weekly payment plans just in case you were not able to pay all at once. I had to sit back and think this through. Would a coach really be able to help me get to full time entrepreneurship? I didn't have money to waste on something that may not work, plus I barely knew this person. Are they even legit? So many questions and not enough answers. OMG! It wasn't long until I realized that I had a fixed mindset when it came to this issue. I wanted to start and grow a business, but I wasn't allowing my mind to be open and grow. I wanted the gold, but was I ready to put in the effort to obtain it? Ummm...nope.

This was all new, exciting and scary at the same time. This is the point where I began to learn if being in business is truly what I wanted. I saw the 'fabulous lives' of professional entrepreneurs on social media, but I didn't understand what they went through to get where they are now. One a day, I was watching a live stream video and the

A New Level Mindset

broadcaster who was a business coach said, "You cannot free your way into entrepreneurship, YOU MUST PAY!" This is when my mind went from fixed to growth. It was time to stop the complaining and get to work building my business. I had to allow myself to be open to what I set out to do. Developing a growth mindset helped to increase my confidence. This *new mindset* got me so confident, that I no longer 'feared' the things that could go wrong as I built my business. I expect things to go wrong, but I know that I will have the confidence to bounce back from it. Now that my mindset was beginning to *shift* toward the likes of entrepreneurship, I discovered more characteristics that I needed to conquer this journey. So, I was back to researching what I needed to get on the right path. While I do have my reservations about not being able to find employment after I graduated from college, I learned to embrace the things I did learn to help me develop on a personal level. I had to stop being so bitter and angry about the situation and be thankful for the skills that I learned. One of those skills was, speaking. In the majority of my classes, PowerPoint presentations were a requirement for homework and projects. I did this for three years, standing in front of my fellow classmates, discussing court cases, amendments and etc. I had no idea that doing this would be preparing me for a future that I couldn't see at that time. I felt that

A New Level Mindset

this was a part of my growth mindset stages; replaying my past to see how I could bring positivity out of what I considered to be bad times and a waste of time.

Once I opened my mind to all the possibilities of becoming an entrepreneur, a series of light bulbs came on in my head. I felt sense of relief, and I was ready to go to the growth mindset of thinking.

Confidence…Umm…Yeah I Need That!

We all have it at some point in our lives. Even as babies and children, we had the confidence to do the things that we wanted. Even if our parents told us not to do it or that we shouldn't do it, we did it anyway. As adults, we become concerned with what people will say or think about us if we do something that is not the norm or if everybody else isn't doing it. When deciding to start a business, many adults feel this way. We sometimes allow the thoughts and sayings of others to control our passions, dreams and goals. There is a quote that says: "Ninety-Seven percent of the people, who give up on their dreams, end up working for the three percent who didn't." Think about that. How determined are you to go after your dreams? Will you allow the talk of others to hold you back? Do you want to be the part of the ninety-seven percent? I sure as hell didn't. I have been at my job for the last eleven years. While I am grateful for this job, I know that it's time for me create a life for myself and my family that will leave a legacy; something to pass on to my grandchildren and great-grandchildren. I had to gain the confidence and unselfishness to understand that this journey to entrepreneurship is no longer about me and what I want. This journey is about the ones who are coming up after me, long after I am gone.

A New Level Mindset

I want to leave something that will be looked at by others; something that others can and will incorporate in their lives. Becoming an entrepreneur could make that possible, but I need to put in the work and claim the abundance. It starts with developing the confidence to do what is needed to get this show on the road. I had to think back to all of those speaking assignments I did in college, and how it helped me to gain the confidence I needed semester after semester. I had to think back to the time I gave a four-minute speech at the graduation in front of 200 people. If I could do that, then I can find the confidence to become a successful entrepreneur. None of what I did was easy, but I did it mainly because I wanted to; not because I had to. I could have easily given up. There were many times that I wanted to, but I no longer had the time to waste on the 'what if's. I had to get fearless and bold. It was time to go after my destiny; scared and all. I was bringing the fear with me.

Look, I understand that it is not easy to all of a sudden break out and start running your own business. It takes practice on top of multiple practices to even get to the point of starting, and that is ok. But if you are serious about the entrepreneurship journey, I highly advise you to just start. It doesn't have to be perfect; just start. Get around people who are positive and want to

A New Level Mindset

help you build the confidence that you need to get yourself up and on your way.

Having confidence and a growth mindset early on before you step into entrepreneurship, will help you succeed during the tough times throughout your journey. If necessary, take a course on personal development, such as public speaking to help you become confident. Ask friends and family to help you practice overcoming any type of fears you have when speaking in front of people. Join a group at your local community center. Begin introducing yourself and get to know others; this will help bring out your confidence. The people in this group may become your first customers.

Jessaca C. Rowe

I increased my confidence by doing live stream video in the beginning of 2017. It was a frightening moment, because I didn't know what people would say; heck, I didn't even think they would even watch. I would get a nauseous feeling in my stomach every time I started a video, but got comfortable as I begin to talk. I stumbled and stuttered over my words, but I hung in there until I was finished or as I saw people leave the video. So far, I done over twenty live stream videos; some great and some not so great. "The best thing I can do is to keep going." This is what you have to tell yourself when you feel like you can't go through it. You have to keep going or you will never know the outcome. If it's good, then Congratulations! If it's

A New Level Mindset

not so great, then try again. The bottom line is to not give up.

Having confidence will be one of the key determining factors as to whether your business will thrive when the going gets tough.

Time to Develop Clarity

Now that I had soaked up all the juicy information about entrepreneurship, I had to get clear on what I wanted to do as an entrepreneur. This was not an easy task. I mean, I am not the type of person who is creative with my hands, I am not the greatest cook/ I don't decorate. I don't have any products or prototypes, BUT I am good at motivating others to take ACTION on something they had been wanting to do for years. Was I going to become a motivational speaker? Hmmm…that sounded like something up my alley. While I was in school, I would post on Facebook my triumphs as I would progress in school. I would also post motivational quotes, and anything I could find to brighten the day of myself and my Facebook friends. Many of them would tell me to keep posting my journey as I was in school, as well as the motivating posts because it helped them to get clear about the path they wanted to take in life. A few of them told me that I should become a motivational speaker. Given that I had prepared and read a speech at my college graduation in front of at least 200 people and received applause throughout my speech, speaking was something that I kept in mind as I started this journey.

If you are considering entrepreneurship, you're going to need to be clear on what you want to provide as an entrepreneur. Is it something that people have always told you that you are good at? Have they even said, "Yeah, you need to start selling the items you create?" Get clear on your passion and the audience you want to serve and provide for. Will what you are offering fill a void or need for your clients? What will you provide to turn your customers into long time clients that will give referrals? Once you are clear on your why and who you are serving, you must focus on beginning the process of developing a plan of action for your soon to be business. You need to be intentional on providing a service that speaks to the people you want to serve.

Research your product or service thoroughly, competition from other entrepreneurs, their strengths, weaknesses, what opportunities you have and what threats that you need to be on the lookout for.

Many of us have more than one thing that we are good at and would like to showcase it all at once. However; if you do have more than one talent, pick the one that will be the most profit producing and then move on to the next.

Clarity is a part of change. The thinking I had ten years ago is nowhere near the thinking I have now; even outside of entrepreneurship. There's a quote by Les Brown that said, "Some of the greatest ideas are in the grave." Boom! That shit hit me like a ton of bricks. It forced me to do more and more research about the type of entrepreneur I wanted to become, and who I wanted to serve. A light bulb came on, and I immediately got to work. Once I got clear on my idea, I began to write this book!

Now ask yourself: What do I need to do to get clear on my "why," and who I want to serve?

QUOTE: "There's nothing quite as intense as the moment of clarity when you suddenly see what's real possible for you."

A New Level Mindset

Focus and Discipline

With the way this world is set up now, it can be challenging to stay focused and disciplined on this journey. The internet is always buzzing. There is a new news story every minute, and we all have personal responsibilities that come before entrepreneurship. As I was figuring out my passion and who I would serve as an entrepreneur, there were times when my focus was just not in it. I still had doubts, and at many times didn't think starting a business was the route for me. I had gone through so much with the focus of trying to start my career path after graduation, that I thought it would be impossible for me to start a business. I knew I had to be focused, but how? "How do I get my mind in position to focus on trying to build something that I'd never done?" Simple. I just had to get it done. You are in control of your life. You determine what you want to do, and what you don't want to do. It's easy to focus on doing what's easy; such as planning a trip, going shopping for new clothes, planning to hang out with friends and going to a job everyday (even though many of us don't want to go to a job). WE DO IT ANYWAY... gotta pay them bills.

If I could focus on those things, I could focus on finding my way to building a business. I had to come up with a few strategies to help me stay focused and disciplined. Now! I am not saying that

I took to them right away. I had to repeat them over and over until it stuck in my head that I could no longer entertain certain things, due to the fact that I needed to concern myself with what was necessary for me to succeed.

My Strategies...

I carve out certain times during the day or night to research ideas or projects, such as Mondays, Wednesdays, Fridays and on the weekends. During the week, I get up an hour before I get ready for work or an hour before I go to bed to research and create content for my social media pages. As for the weekends, I'll work all day on Saturdays and few hours on Sunday. While at work, I would use my breaks and lunch hour to listen to relevant podcasts or YouTube videos and take notes. I bring my lunch, so there is no need to leave the office to grab something to eat. I get an hour for lunch, so I use my time wisely.

I also listen to audio on the way to work and on the way home from work. When I get to a stop light, I grab my pocket size notebook and pen to take notes. Yeah...It's that serious for me.

These were the 1st of many things I needed to do to get my ideas in focus. I read a quote on the internet that said, "Starve your distractions and feed your focus." My distractions are of course cable TV, Netflix, the radio and random videos and posts on social media. In the beginning, I would frequently visit these distractions and be mad Monday morning on my way to work, because I was not where I wanted to be in building my business. So, I had to stop with the bullshit and get my focus all the way together. I had to ask myself did I want to be sitting in traffic for the rest of my life working a job that I have outgrown. NOPE!

While maintaining focus and discipline has its challenges on this journey, you cannot let that deter you from staying on track. When a life situation comes at you, deal with it as needed and get back to work. You have to nurture the business process in order for it to grow into the success that you know it can be. You have to become confident in the decisions and choices that you make as you are in the early developmental stages. You need to set up times in which you can work on the necessities: making phone calls, meeting with a mentor or coach, doing continued research and etc.

Your focus cannot be on activities that do not correlate with the focus you have already put in place to birth your business. You are going to have to miss out to come up. Period! Pointblank! If you are serious about what you are embarking on, then missing out will not faze you.

I love inspiring quotes; so anytime I feel like I'm falling off, I find an inspiring quote to pick me up and help me get disciplined:

A New Level Mindset

"Through discipline comes freedom."

I had to remember my "WHY," and part of my "WHY" is to help aspiring entrepreneurs get their ideas out of their heads and start taking action on their ideas by providing them with goal achieving strategies. I have to keep my mind disciplined and focused, so that I'll be able to serve, inspire and motivate as I was called to do.

I asked a few aspiring entrepreneurs how they stay focused as they build their businesses: Arthur Brown III of *ABIII Photography* located in Los Angeles, California says: "By seeking more information, reading up on technical intel about new equipment. I would say getting new information keeps me focused. Research, Research, Research."

DeWanda Davis of *Yesterday's Treasures* located in Mobile, Alabama says: "I stay focused by encouraging and talking to myself, connecting and reaching out to my "support system" to get additional words of encouragement."

Now ask yourself: "What can you do to get your mind focused? What are you willing to "turn off" to get your focus and discipline in tune?"

The Power of Support

A New Level Mindset

When I started my journey, I had verbal encouragement such as, "Hooray, you go girl, that's awesome, I am proud of you, keep up the good work!" That is great support, but you also need support from a circle of people who you can physically talk with on a needed basis. You cannot fully embark on this journey alone. The support system you choose will determine your success.

Reach out to friends who you know to be genuine, and who will keep it 100% with you at all times as you begin to set up your business. To those who have always been supportive of you no matter what or how often you have mentioned your business ideas to them. You feel comfortable talking to them about anything, and you know they won't judge you.

    I am proud to say that my friends have been supportive throughout my journey. I have friends who encourage me when I talk to them about the challenges I face on this journey. I am grateful for them, but nobody could motivate me more than my BFF Danisha Tanner. She would get on me so tough, when I would speak in a negative tone about my challenges. When I was going through depression and anxiety, she would send me bible verses every evening. Unfortunately, she passed away in February 2016 just as I was about to thoroughly dive deep into the process of entrepreneurship. Her death was a deep wound for me. We had known each other since the 8th grade. We became good friends in high school and went on to become best friends after high school. We lost contact with each other a few times after high school as we were still living with our parents and technology with cell phones and computers were not as advanced as they are today. However, we managed to always find each other. As we got older, we grew closer and looked to each other as sisters. We were present for each other's wedding, also when we had children and other life changing events in our lives. In July 2015, she was diagnosed with cancer. She went through chemo and did everything she needed to do to fight the illness. I would go and see her every time she went in the hospital for chemo. We would pray, laugh and talk about the future. We just knew after she had her last round of chemo that she would be ok. A few weeks before she died, I found an old picture of us. I sent it to her in a text message hoping to brighten her spirits. She replied, "I love you." Tears rolled down my eyes when I read the text. It indicated to me that she knew she was not going to survive much longer. After her death, I was crushed. I had lost my best friend. Damn. I could not believe it. I was sad and angry. Why her? Why my friend? Why did this have to happen to her? I shut down everything that I was working on as far as entrepreneurship. I felt like I could go on no longer. After a few months, a Facebook memory from of our conversation we had a year prior popped up on my page. I made a motivational post about my entrepreneur journey and she responded, "Let the spirit of God guide you." When I saw that memory, I knew that was her talking to me, telling me to get back up and get on my grind. WHEW! To this day, I feel that she comes to me in different forms that encourage me to move forward. True friends are necessary on this journey. Take a good look at who truly has your back. How are they encouraging you to stay focused on your dreams and goals?

Your professional circle should consist of accountability partner(s), coaches, mentors, influencers and experts.

Jessaca C. Rowe

If you don't already have a professional circle, create one. I found many professional groups on Facebook, Meetup.com and Instagram. One particular group on Facebook; "Screw the 9-5," is a great group that helped me to get a sneak peek into what it's like to be a full-time entrepreneur. There were people who shared their wins and losses. They sought advice from this group and many times got the help they needed; they even made business connections with others. Local networking events and conferences are great ways to meet your professional friends. 'Heal a Woman to Heal a Nation,' was the 1st in person conference I attended to meet like-minded women. We were a group full of women who were entrepreneurs and aspiring entrepreneurs. We were all supportive of one another. We called each other "sisters" as we spoke to each other about our goals and dreams, and where we saw ourselves in the next 2-3 years. Surround yourself with people who talk about and ACT on their visions and ideas.

I love this quote as it relates to support. I tweaked it a little bit: "Behind every successful person is a tribe of other successful people who has their back."

Who is on your team?

A New Level Mindset

Ready...Set...Goals!

It can be challenging to complete goals due to the happenings of LIFE, but we must stay focused and continue to set goals. I like to think of goal setting as my ticket to the next level of launching my business.

There are a few internet influencers that I have come across who say setting goals don't work. They say that you should just, "go for it." I agree in a sense that you absolutely just go for it; but at the same time, you also have to do what works best for you as you build your business. Goal setting has absolutely worked for me. Once I complete a goal, I feel closer to my dream. I feel a sense of greatness and satisfaction, as I have made a commitment to following through with what I set out to do. I am getting myself to the next level, each time I complete a goal.

There are many ways to set goals. You have to find a way that is comfortable for you; a way that you know that you will be able to follow through with your goals.

The classic way of setting goals is known as **S.M.A.R.T.** This stands for **Specific, Measurable, Attainable, Relevant and Time-Bound.** The outcome of using this goal setting method is to ensure that the goals you set will consistently help you achieve higher levels as you grow your business.

Here is the breakdown of how this method works:

SPECIFIC: What, when, where and how. This goes back to clarity on what product or service you will provide, to whom and how will you get the word out.

MEASURABLE: How much time will you put into working on your business? Ex: 30-45 mins a day on creating content, reading relevant books, listening to podcasts and helpful YouTube videos.

ATTAINABLE: How will you make ease of or access to achieve your goals?

RELEVANT: Do the activities you are working on in an average day reflect with the goals you have set for yourself?

TIME-BOUND: What time frame have you given yourself to set these goals? Three months? Six months or Twelve months? You can also break them down on a weekly basis.

Recently, I learned of another method by Vishen Lakhiani. He is an entrepreneur, author and speaker. He is the founder and CEO of *Mindvalley,* and the author of *'The Code of the Extraordinary Mind.'* When it comes to business and setting goals for ourselves, he recommends that we ask ourselves these 3 questions:

1. What do I want for my business?
2. How do I have to achieve this?
3. What contributions will this provide?

A New Level Mindset

My answer: I want for my business to be the premier source for aspiring entrepreneurs. It will provide the necessary resources and access to expert advice from established entrepreneurs. This will be done by creating helpful content and reaching out to experts who will provide advice and services. This will empower aspiring entrepreneurs by helping them overcome their fears of starting their business, and develop a new level mindset as it relates to entrepreneurship.

Within this paragraph, I am able to breakdown attainable goals. I know what I want my business to be, so this gives me clarity. I know how I will be able to achieve this, and I know what contributions my business will have in the world.

Jessaca C. Rowe

I'll review my goals on a daily basis and ensure that I am making strides to complete my goals. I'll set no more than five goals to complete within a month. Whichever goals that I don't complete, will simply get push to the following month and so on. The overall goal is to persevere through each month until my goals are fully complete.

Look, entrepreneurship is new territory. It's scary to think of quitting your full-time job of which we feel is "safe" and to get out there in the world and ask people to support your dream. That's a big deal! Many of us were not taught how to create our own source of income; heck, we didn't even know it was possible. Do not get discouraged, if you are not able to complete the goals you've set in a certain period of time. If you get stuck, go back to your support circle. Ask them for suggestions on how you can move forward. Remember, you cannot do this alone. There will be times that you need help. Do not be ashamed at this point or any point on this journey. As long you can get up every morning, you still have a chance to complete your goals.

QUOTE: "Setting goals is the first step in turning the invisible to the visible."

Creativity is Key!

    I love powerful quotes. I share many of them on Facebook and my audience loves them, so I decided to create a guide called, 'Quotes to Keep You Woke.' I showed it to a few people, and they loved it. I also do a weekly podcast called 'Three Quotes to Keep You Woke.' In doing this, my goals were to see if my audience preferred the guide or the podcast. Many preferred the podcast, because it is easier to access from their phone and listen to it in the car or while they are doing chores and etc. I also play around with Instagram using the fifteen second timer to deliver a word of inspiration to my followers. Your ideas matter! You have to be in tune and keep up to date with the trends in your field. Along with giving your clients what they want and need, be open to all the suggestions you receive. I am not saying compromise your values and beliefs, but you will need to listen to your clients and ask them what they want. If you become stuck with your creativity, go back to your success circle and ask for assistance. You will need to come up with creative ways to keep your product and or service fresh and appealing to your clients. Let's say your product or service is great. Everyone loves it, but the spark for it is no longer as hype as it was when it was first presented. How do you get people to remain interested in the products or services you provide? You have to come up with "ask what you need" sessions, and then create a product or service around that. To come up with topics or ideas, surf the internet to see what people are asking for. I think creativity is the beauty of entrepreneurship. You can be as creative as you want to be! It's your ideas and your business. There is no boss or manager telling you that your ideas suck, and them embarrassing you in front of your coworkers. You get to choose if it sucks and be ok with it. When those brilliant ideas come to you at 3am, get up and write them down. Ask people from your success circle to critique and evaluate it. Overall, have fun with the process. Keep going until you get it. Take a break if necessary, but by all means do not give up. Think outside the box as you build your business. What if Mark Zuckerberg didn't follow through with his ideas? What if the same was with Steve Jobs, Albert Einstein and etc? What if they said, "Nah, this will never work," and took no action.

What idea have you always wanted to introduce to the world?

QUOTE: "You can't use up creativity. The more you use, the more you have." ~Maya Angelou

A New Level Mindset

Becoming a Risk Taker

We take risks every day when we leave our homes. We risk getting a flat tire or missing the bus on the way to work, because we wanted that cup of coffee from Starbucks. We also risk having our credit/debit card information stolen through the electronic portals at the grocery store or mall. We go about our lives on a daily basis to get the things we need and want. We mostly never question our daily actions. We just do them without fear, because we don't expect anything to go wrong.

Many have doubts about entrepreneurship, because it can be scary and risky. It is reported that many businesses fail during or after their first year.

Yet, many people still take the risk to start their businesses, and they are successful. So how is it that some people are successful in business, and some are not? Well, some are willing to take risks in their business and some are not. Most people are fearful, and most people are not. If you want to go higher in your business, you MUST be willing to take a calculated risk and let go of the fear of what can go wrong.

Let's say you've been in business as a candle maker for about a year. You make scented organic candles. An organic company you like has heard about your candles. On account of one of its employees, they made a purchase at your booth at a flea market, and they are well pleased with your product. A person from that company gets in touch with you and wants you to talk about a partnership. You are excited! Bursting with joy and tears! You think, 'Finally, this is a way to increase my business and profits!' You agree to have a meeting with them. Cool, right? Ok, so three days before the meeting, they contact you and ask you to come prepared to give a speech to the company's shareholders, a few managers and executives. Speech? There was no mention of a speech in the previous phone call.

You are terrified of speaking. The only speaking you've done about your product is to family, friends and the customers you interact with at the weekly flea market. This changes the whole game now. How are you gonna pull this off? You really like this company and you would love to do business with them, but speaking in front of a large audience is not your thing. Should you choose to miss out on this meeting, because you fear speaking to large crowds? If so, then you will lose out on an opportunity to improve your business and take it to the next level. You have to overcome your fears and take the risk to find out what's on the other side. Les Brown said, "If you don't take the risk, you won't grow."

Once I found out that you cannot "free" your way into entrepreneurship and began paying for coaching programs, I was able to understand the importance of paying to get to the next level.

A New Level Mindset

It's just like that online game, Candy Crush. You were given a certain number of free attempts to pass to the next level. If you used up all the attempts before you were able to complete the level, you would have to wait a certain amount of time before you were given new free chances. You could ask a Facebook friend to give you an attempt, or you could take a risk by paying to get to the next level of the game. I took a risk and enrolled in a $1000 coaching program for 10 weeks. The name of the program was called, "Monetize Everything." This program showed me how to use my gifts, talents and skills to create multiple products and services that would translate into multiple streams of income. The program was great, but the spending $1000 was risky. I had never spent that much money on a program taught by a person that I met on the internet, but I felt that I really needed this class to help me bring out my creativity and continue on my journey. I had paid more than a thousand dollars for three years to a school to obtain a bachelor's degree and get a better paying job. Well if you read the introduction, then you know how that turned out. The course was definitely worth it, and I would take a risk and pay for any course that is needed to help me succeed in entrepreneurship. You have to do thorough research when it comes to purchasing courses and hiring a coach to help you get to the next level in your business.

A New Level Mindset

That is what entrepreneurship is about: taking risks and doing what others won't do. Make sure it's a person whom you are familiar with. If they are recommended, that's even better. Make sure this person aligns with your process of starting your business.

READ!

Books! Yes! Books have helped me tremendously on this journey. Thanks to the many recommendations of great books by a few of the entrepreneurs I follow on social media, I was able to open my mind to all that is possible for me in entrepreneurship. Dawniel Winningham's book: *'The Quit Conspiracy,'* details the difference from working a job to creating your OWN job and working for yourself. Ashlan Rae's book: *'She's an Overnight Success and Other Stupid Sh!t People Say,'* refers to the breakdown of what it actually takes to develop and maintain your business. Both of these books; (as well as mine), are great starters for aspiring entrepreneurs. Other books I would recommend are: *The Power of Broke* by Daymond John, *How to Win Friends and Influence People* by Dale Carnegie and *Abundance NOW!* by Lisa Nichols.

Reading books in the entrepreneur industry helps to keep me up-to-date on current trends which are subject to change at a moment's notice. I can read all the books I want, but the end result is to apply the knowledge that I read. There is no other way around it. Find a reading club in your area or online. When you read books along with others and gather to discuss what was read, you begin to expand your mind to the opinions of others. You may not wholly agree with what they have to say; but in some ways, their opinions can be helpful to you in deciding on what direction you want to go next in your business.

Once you begin to read and understand the game of entrepreneurship, you will go on to explore other ways to increase your income. I am currently looking into real estate investing and stock market investing. I purchased the book, *Stock Market Investing for Beginners.* This book was written by business experts at *Tyco Press.* Tyco Press specializes in creating accessible hand books that simplify even the most complex topics, so that readers can easily expand their knowledge on topics.

Jessaca C. Rowe

By participating in these forms of investments; as well as my business, I am will be able to grow my wealth and build my legacy. I understand that this is a huge risk, but it's one that I am willing to take. I've played it safe for a long time. I did what was normal by society's standards. I followed the status quo and did what the 97% did. How is that working out for me? Eh...it's ok. BUT now that I know that I am able to achieve more than just the status quo, it's GAME ON! I will continue to say that it's not easy, but I am willing to give it all I got and fail. I am willing to give it all I've got and fail again. As long as I keep going, my abundance will come through, right?

Set Backs Happen for a Come Back!

Get ready, because it's gonna come. Yes, the setbacks! Embrace them and look forward to them. Always have a backup plan when a problem arises. (Give simple examples). You may launch a product and need a certain amount of people to sign up, but only half sign up, what do you do? Would this be a setback for you?

Embrace the difficulties on the journey. Don't be scared of making mistakes, because you will. Always look for opportunities to learn more. Stay driven. Keep your "why" and goals at the forefront of your mind. When I am having troubles moving forward on this journey, I go back and look at the concepts that I have written in this book. When it comes to my "trouble," which concept do I need to reference so that I may move forward? Do I need to change my goals? Is my confidence up to par? Did I allow my mindset to drift back to a fixed mindset? Please understand and know that this is perfectly normal. You will not have all of the answers. As long as you seek "wise counsel," you should be fine. As long as you don't give up, you should be fine. As long as you don't allow the opinions of other to deter you, you should be fine.

This may sound crazy, but I think setbacks are the best thing that can happen in entrepreneurship. A setback can allow you to come back stronger than before. I think of it as you not being at your best the first go around. So, the setback happened for you to be even better than before.

There are many famous people who had plenty of setbacks, but refused to allow it stop them. Walt Disney was told that he was not creativity enough and that he didn't have enough imagination. Oprah Winfrey was fired from her job as a journalist, because she was too emotional when reporting a news story. Harry Potter author J.K. Rowling was rejected over a dozen times. One publisher decided to publish the book, but told her that she would need to get a job because she wouldn't make a lot of money writing children's books. These examples are proof that it's possible to overcome setbacks. We must understand that many successful people we see went through times in their lives when they thought it wasn't possible to become successful. Their success is part of their belief system. Despite their setbacks, they didn't give up. They believed in their passions and dreams. As an aspiring entrepreneur, I have also developed this belief system. I know that my success is entirely up to me. I am my own rescue. If I give up because of a few setbacks, why should anyone else believe in me?

I read a quote that said: "Setbacks are guidelines, not stop signs" Right?! That's how you

A New Level Mindset

have to look at it. It's merely a guideline to get you back on track.

Final Thoughts

Entrepreneurship is a lifestyle. You will need to change your life and adjust to this new life. You may lose friends, and become distance from family members. This is the REAL DEAL! If you want to live the lifestyle of freedom and make as much money as you need and want without any restrictions (such as a job), you will have to work your ass off. There are not secrets or magic tricks, just systems, strategies, coaching, late nights, early mornings, tears, sweat and probably some blood.

I took me three and a half years to fully understand what the characteristics of an entrepreneur fully entail. I discovered that truly having a growth mindset and become a person who is 100% percent determined to push forward; no matter the obstacles is what matters most. Look, I know unforeseen events happen in our lives. Some of the events will shake us to the core, leaving us to wonder if we can push through with our goals and dreams. In the end, that decision is totally up to us. We make the choices as to what we want to happen in our lives. Many of the choices are not easy, and it can be a struggle to continue on our journey. This; my friends, will be well worth it.

Thomas Edison said: "Our greatest weakness lies in giving up. The most certain way to succeed is always to just try one more time."

A New Level Mindset

Let's stay connected:

Facebook:

https://www.facebook.com/jessacarowe

Instagram: project_empower_me

Website: projectempowerme.com

End

www.ingramcontent.com/pod-product-compliance
Lightning Source LLC
Chambersburg PA
CBHW071227160426
43196CB00012B/2436